TENNESSEE WOMEN
FOR THE VOTE

TENNESSEE WOMEN FOR THE VOTE:

A Suffrage Play, 1920

by

B. Ayne Cantrell

Part of this play was originally published in *Tennessee Women of Vision and Courage*, 2013. Used by permission.

Copyright © 2019 Tennessee Women Project

All Rights Reserved

ISBN: 978-0-578-61202-7

Library of Congress Control Number: 2019920354

Womens Equity Foundation
Maryville, Tennessee

We must remember the past, hold fast to the present, and build for the future. If you stand in our accepted place today, it is because some woman had to fight yesterday. We should be ashamed to stand on ground won by women in the past without making an effort to honor them by winning a higher and wider field for the future. It is a debt we owe.

—Sue Shelton White (1926)

CONTENTS

Preface

Tennessee Women for the Vote is a rally for woman suffrage set in Nashville, Tennessee, on June 25, 1920, fifty-four days before the Tennessee General Assembly voted to ratify the Nineteenth Amendment to the US Constitution. Tennessee was the thirty-sixth and final state needed to ratify the amendment, which gave American women the vote.

While all participants named in the play are actual historical figures, their coming together at this time and place is imaginary. Speeches are authentic, but much has been rearranged, and the historical period has been condensed for dramatic effect. Lide Meriwether, for example, retired from the struggle for woman's vote in 1900 after she had been a leader in the movement in Tennessee for over twenty years. She died in 1913 and could not have shared the stage with Kenny, White, Allen, and Dudley in 1920 as depicted in the play.

Another departure from history is the rally's inclusion of women of color. Given White suffragists' fear that association with African American women would mean a loss of support for woman suffrage, it is unlikely that J. Frankie Pierce and Mattie E. Coleman would have been asked to speak at the rally as they do in the play. Their participation, however, recognizes that Black women leaders understood the importance of winning the vote, and, as historian Rosalyn Terborg-Penn points out, Black women "contributed significantly to the passage of the Nineteenth Amendment."[1]

Also pertinent to African American women's roles in the play is the rally's setting. If there were any city in Tennessee where Black and White women could come together to rally for the vote, it would have been Nashville. By 1919 when Tennessee granted women partial suffrage (they could vote in municipal and presidential elections), Nashville was the only city in the state where biracial alliances were formed to register women voters and to support the Citizen Party's progressive reforms. A sign that the alliance had been successful was the Tennessee General Assembly's

---

1. Rosalyn Terborg-Penn, *African American Women in the Struggle for the Vote, 1850-1920* (Bloomington: U of Indiana P, 1998) 11.

passage of a bill creating the Tennessee Vocational School for Colored Girls in 1921. Black women's gains, however, were short lived. Terborg-Penn explains that Black women in the South were robbed of their ballots by White political supremacy and thus were "disenfranchised in less than a decade after the Nineteenth Amendment enfranchised them."[2]

The passage of the Nineteenth Amendment to the US Constitution in 1920 marked the end of a seventy-two-year struggle for woman suffrage. In 2020 as we celebrate the centennial of the amendment's passage and the right of all American citizens to vote, we recognize courageous Tennessee women who, at great risk to themselves, stepped out of traditional boundaries of home and race and entered public life to fight for women's right to vote. We acknowledge the debt we owe these women. Their examples remind us that our work is not done. Their stories spur us on to continue the fight for equal rights for all American women.

---

2. Ibid., 12.

Tennessee Women
for the Vote

Cast of Characters[3]
In order of appearance

Catherine Talty Kenny	A suffragist platform speaker from Nashville. Kenny (age 46) is a good public speaker and reader of her audience.
Suffragist Leader	A vivacious female spectator who leads the audience in chants and applause for the suffragist speakers.
Sue Shelton White	A suffragist platform speaker from Jackson. White (youngest speaker at age 33) is defiant and speaks aggressively.
Martha Elizabeth Moore Allen	A suffragist platform speaker from Memphis. Allen (age 71) is an eloquent speaker who has had much practice speaking for woman suffrage.
Heckler 1	Anti-suffragist male spectator.

---

3. Biographies of suffragists may be found after the Property List.

Lide Smith Meriwether	A suffragist platform speaker from Memphis. Meriwether (a lifelong proponent of equal rights for women) speaks with the confidence of a seasoned political activist.
Anne Dallas Dudley	A suffragist platform speaker from Nashville. Dudley (age 44) is known for her beauty and charming wit, which she displays in her speeches.
John Jacob Vertrees	Nashville attorney and opponent of woman suffrage. Vertrees (age 70) speaks loudly with masculine authority.
Josephine Pearson	Anti-suffragist from Monteagle. Pearson (age 52) speaks with contempt for the suffragists because she believes she is doing God's work.
Heckler 2	Anti-suffragist female spectator.
Hecklers 3, 4	Anti-suffragist male spectators.
Mattie E. Coleman	An African American suffragist from Nashville. Coleman (age 50) is not intimidated by the White audience and speaks confidently.
J. Frankie Pierce	An African American suffragist from Nashville. Pierce (age 56) speaks proudly as one who is sure of her position and self-worth.

Scene

Ryman Auditorium, Nashville, Tennessee

Time

June 25, 1920

A podium stands center stage with three straight chairs at stage left and two straight chairs at stage right. These are flanked by banners (purple, white, and gold), which read "VOTES FOR WOMEN!"

As audience attendees arrive, suffragists give those in favor of the woman vote yellow roses to wear and anti-suffragists give those against the woman vote red roses to wear, and they encourage the audience to participate in the rally. The audience includes longtime supporters of the woman vote JOSEPH HANOVER, member of the Tennessee House of Representatives, and US Congressman THETUS W. SIMS (both are dressed in period costumes) and suffragists J. FRANKIE PIERCE and MATTIE E. COLEMAN (dressed in period costumes). They carry signs that read "Colored Women for the Vote" and "Negro Women are Suffragists, Too." Another audience member is SUFFRAGIST LEADER

1

(dressed in a period costume) who acts as a cheerleader for pro-suffrage spectators. She hands out suffrage literature before the rally begins.

Also, among spectators are anti-suffragists JOHN VER-TREES and JOSEPHINE PEARSON. They are dressed in period costumes and carry signs that read, "Women's vote will feminize men" and "Women belong in the home, not in the ballot box!" They are joined by HECKLERS 1, 2, 3, & 4 (anti-suffragist men and women dressed in period costumes) who interrupt the speakers and often "boo" suffrage speeches throughout the rally. One of the anti-suffragists hands out anti-suffrage literature before the rally begins.

Wearing white dresses with yellow sashes, speakers KENNY, DUDLEY, MERIWETHER, WHITE, and ALLEN march into the hall (in this order) and down to stage left carrying signs and chanting slogans: "Votes are women's rights!" "No more tyranny!" "We demand the vote!" "Women are men's equal!" "Give us the vote!" Supporters chanting slogans and carrying signs trail these speakers (the number of these supporters can be as many as the production allows). The supporters take seats in the audience as speakers march on to the stage. The Ryman Auditorium will be hot in late June, so speakers and their supporters carry fans with suffrage slogans—these they occasionally use to cool off during the rally.

As the speakers march to the stage, suffragists in the audience applaud and shout chants. Hecklers boo.

When the speakers reach the stage, Kenny stands at her seat far SR of podium and Dudley stands in front of her chair L of Kenny. Meriwether stands in front of first chair SL of podium, White stands in front of chair L of Meriwether, and Allen stands in front of the chair L of White. They raise their signs and shout their slogans.

The audience cheers and applauds. When cheers die down, the speakers put signs behind chairs and sit, except for Kenny who goes to the podium to introduce the rally.

(Before she begins speaking, Kenny waits at the podium until the audience quietens and the other speakers are settled in their seats. She looks over the audience and begins.)

KENNY

I am Catherine Talty Kenny, and on behalf of the Tennessee Equal Suffrage Association and the Tennessee League of Women Voters, I say *(she raises her arm and encourages the audience and platform speakers to join with her, which they do)*: Votes for Women! Votes for Women! Votes for Women! Votes for Women! . . .

(A few boos are heard from the anti-suffragists in the audience, but these are drowned out by the audience's overwhelming support of suffrage for women.)

Thank you for your support of woman suffrage. Today, we need you more than ever, for in Tennessee we stand on the precipice for the woman vote. Governor Albert Roberts has recently announced that he will convene a special session of the Tennessee General Assembly in August—just a few days from now—to consider ratification of the US Constitution's Nineteenth Amendment. The constitutional amendment will guarantee women the right to vote in <u>all</u> elections throughout our great nation.

(Cheers and applause from the platform speakers and audience.)

Thirty-five states have already ratified the amendment. We need only Tennessee's ratification to make the woman vote the law of the land!

SUFFRAGIST LEADER

(Suffragist Leader chants, "Number 36 . . . Number 36" . . . and audience members join in.)

KENNY

(Waits for the chant to die down and speaks.)

I share the stage with suffragists who have spent years campaigning in Tennessee for the woman vote. We have founded suffrage societies across the state in Knoxville, Nashville, Morristown, Chattanooga, Memphis, and Jackson.[4] We have become outspoken activists at a time when it is thought by many that a woman's place is in the home, and that, like children, we should be seen but not heard. We are here today to say that WE WILL BE HEARD!

SUFFRAGIST LEADER

(Leads audience in chant "We will be heard. . . . We will be heard . . . ." *As they shout, some of the suffragists get exceedingly rowdy as if to turn on the anti-suffragists (who are booing) and strike them with their signs.)*

KENNY

(Raises her hand to calm the suffragists and shouts...)

---

4. A. Elizabeth Taylor, "Tennessee The Thirty-Sixth State," *Votes for Women! The Woman Suffrage Movement in Tennessee, the South, and the Nation,* ed. Marjorie Spruill Wheeler (Knoxville: U of Tennessee, 1955) 54.

Calm down. Please calm down. We will be heard, BUT WE WILL NOT STOOP TO VIOLENCE FOR THE CAUSE! That being said, we have with us today a true revolutionary heroine on the behalf of women, a woman who has picketed the White House and risked everything for the woman vote—Sue Shelton White of Jackson, Tennessee. While some of you may not approve, Miss White has the distinction of being the only Tennessean to be arrested for her suffrage work.[5] She will tell us of her ordeal.

(Kenny leads the audience in applause for Miss White as she approaches the podium. They shake hands. Kenny takes her seat far SR of podium, White prepares to speak but is interrupted.)

HECKLER 1

(Stands and shouts.)

Go back home, Sue. We don't want your kind in Nashville! Go back to Jackson!

---

5. On the topic of radical suffrage demonstrations, according to A. Elizabeth Taylor, *The Woman Suffrage Movement in Tennessee* (New York: Bookman, 1957), women suffragists of the South, including those in Tennessee, did not approve of practices such as picketing the White House. They thought such demonstrations were "unworthy of southern women" 56.

WHITE

Sir, I will <u>not</u> go home until every woman in Tennessee and in the United States has the vote. Should not all who are governed by the law, and that includes women, have a voice in making the law? We women have too long been denied this right.

(Applause and boos.)

And I will not go home because women before me did not go home. In July 1848, an equal rights convention was held in Seneca Falls, New York, to discuss the rights of women. Convention attendees resolved that "Woman is man's equal—was intended to be so by the Creator, and the highest good of the race demands that she should be recognized as such."[6] They said, "The history of mankind is a history of repeated injuries and usurpations on the part of man toward woman, having in direct object the establishment of an absolute tyranny over her." In response to this tyranny, the women of the Seneca Falls convention resolved

---

6. White's quotations from the Seneca Falls convention are excerpted from "Declaration of Sentiments and Resolutions of the Woman's Rights Convention, Held at Seneca Falls, 19–20 July 1848," *The Selected Papers of Elizabeth Cady Stanton & Susan B. Anthony*, vol. 1 (New Brunswick: Rutgers U, 1997), The Elizabeth Cady Stanton & Susan B. Anthony Papers Project, 7 May 2012 < http://ecssba.rutgers.edu/docs/seneca.html/>.

that it was the "duty of the women of this country to secure to themselves their sacred right of the elective franchise." Now in 1920—seventy-two years later—we women still do not enjoy the right of the ballot box.

SUFFRAGIST LEADER

(Stands and leads audience in chant "Women's vote NOW" . . . "Women's vote NOW.")

WHITE

(Waiting until the chant dies down, White continues.)

The women of Seneca Falls did not go home, and by their examples, neither will I. Mrs. Kenny asked me to share my story of being arrested for my suffrage work.[7]

Two years ago, I moved to Washington, DC, and joined the great crusade for the woman vote led by the NWP, the National Woman Party. One of our objectives was to secure President Woodrow Wilson's support of a constitutional

---

7. The story of White's arrest is found in Elaine Weiss, *The Woman's Hour: The Great Fight to Win the Vote* (New York: Penguin, 2019) and in Carol Lynn Yellin and Janann Sherman, *The Perfect 36: Tennessee Delivers Woman Suffrage* (Oak Ridge: Iris, 1998). Weiss points out that White's act of burning the president in effigy was condemned by Tennessee suffragists of a less radical bent.

amendment that would give women the vote. The president appeared to support such an amendment. He told French feminists attending the Paris Peace Conference that he favored women's enfranchisement around the world and he often spoke of freedom and democracy for all, but in 1919 when the amendment was to come up for another vote in congress, the President did not push Democratic Senators to vote for its approval. To get the president's attention, members of the NWP picketed the White House. There we burned the president's hypocritical words on pieces of paper in small bonfires we called "Watchfires of Freedom." But the president continued to ignore us. Soon it appeared we would lose the Senate vote. We had to take a more <u>drastic</u> approach.

HECKLER 1

(Heckler 1 loudly boos, but members of the audience, now intent on listening, shush him. Sympathetic spectators and speakers are visibly shocked by White's acts of protest and moved by her suffering at the hands of authorities.)

To get the president's attention, I was asked to lead a large group of suffragists from twenty-two states on February 9, 1919, in a march to the White House to rally for woman suffrage, the climax of which was so radical that the police would have no choice but to arrest us. That we would be arrested was certain, but we also ran the risk of being attacked by gangs of rowdy men and boys who always harassed us at suffrage events. Was I brave enough to march on the White House and conduct the unforgivable deed? Friends back home in Tennessee discouraged me, fearing for my safety. Ultimately, I agreed to lead the march.

Our march to the White House began at four-thirty on a Sunday afternoon, the eve of the Senate vote. About seventy-five women walked in silence as NWP colleague Louisine Havemeyer held high the American flag and others carried banners that said, "The President is responsible for the betrayal of American Womanhood" and "President Wilson is deceiving the world." Some carried the Watchfire urn and kerosene-soaked logs for the fire. As we marched along, I began to have self-doubts again. What would my family and friends think of me? Are we going too far? Is such an act appropriate for me, a woman? The closer we got to the White House, the more quickly my heart beat.

Then we arrived. Louisine spoke first. In every Anglo-Saxon country in the world, she said, including our mortal enemy of the last war, Germany, women are enfranchised. But not in the United States. While she spoke, the fire was lit, and I stepped forward with a paper doll drawn in the image of President Wilson. This time not just the President's words would burn. There was a flash of fire as I dropped the President's effigy into the flame and shouted, "We burn not the effigy of the President of a free people, but the leader of an autocratic party organization whose tyrannical power holds millions of women in political slavery."

Almost immediately, policemen rushed me and roughly pushed me into a waiting patrol wagon. I was shaken but proud. I and others were taken to the Old Workhouse jail and thrown into dark, rat-infested cells. We slept on damp straw beds covered by cockroaches and endured cold the severity of which I have never experienced. As planned, we would not eat the wormy bread they set before us. Instead, we went on a hunger strike, and in five days, we were released.[8]

Congress did not pass the Nineteenth Amendment the next day after the rally as we had hoped, but it did four months later in June 1919, setting the stage for the battle for state ratification we have today in Tennessee. Burning the president in effigy was "the most difficult thing I was ever asked to do, the greatest sacrifice I have ever made, and nothing but the deepest conviction could have moved me to do it."

---

8. Though severe, White's treatment by the police was less dreadful as that of other NWP members at other times. NWP President Alice Paul, for example, spent six months in jail and was force fed three times a day through a tube pushed down her throat. Yellin and Sherman report in *The Perfect 36*, "In all, 218 women from twenty-six states were arrested, ninety-seven of whom went to prison" 35.

(She turns to Kenny.) Mrs. Kenny, I am honored to have served the cause this way.

(Lots of cheering. White raises her hand to quieten the audience so that she can finish her speech.)

We southern women have lagged behind our northern sisters in the movement to win the right to vote, but Tennessee can be proud that we have taken a more active part among the southern states in this crusade. Present with me on the platform are Tennessee women who have campaigned for woman suffrage. Among them is Mrs. Martha Elizabeth Allen of Memphis who has become known as the "grandmother of the Memphis League of Women Voters."[9] We are honored to have her among us and invite her to come forward to tell us about the suffrage work here in Tennessee.

(While the audience applauds, Allen comes forward and shakes White's hand. White retires to her seat. Allen goes to the podium.)

---

9. Paula F. Casey, "Four Prominent Tennessee Suffragists," *Tennessee Women of Vision and Courage*, eds. Charlotte Crawford and Ruth Johnson Smiley (North Charleston: CreateSpace, 2013) 49.

ALLEN

Thank you, Miss White. One of the most important functions of our campaign for woman suffrage has been to place woman suffrage literature before the public. "We have tried novel ways of distributing our leaflets. We visit railway depots and place them in the timetable holders. We often mingle among crowds formed by some parade or collected by some unusual occurrence and hand out leaflets.[10] These are efforts to build public support for the Nineteenth Amendment, which says that no American citizen will be denied the vote because of their sex.

(At the mention of the word "sex," several members of the audience are obviously offended. Allen is somewhat perturbed by the ruckus her use of the word "sex" has created, but continues her speech.)

We believe that if you understand the need for woman suffrage, you will favor it. Today, a member of the association has been passing among you with suffrage information that I hope you will read.

(While Allen continues her speech, Suffragist Leader stands and waves a handful of leaflets to see if there is anyone who

10. Report of the Tennessee Equal Suffrage Association, 1910, quoted in Taylor, *Woman Suffrage* 31.

needs a copy. Some members of the audience raise their hands, and she delivers the leaflets to them.)

One of the most popular pieces of literature that we distribute is entitled *Perhaps,* written by Carrie Chapman Catt, President of the National American Woman Suffrage Association. Soon Mrs. Catt will be in Nashville to join in our fight for Tennessee's ratification of the Nineteenth Amendment.

(Many boos from anti-suffragists in the audience.)

I will now read a portion of Mrs. Catt's remarks. She says,

Perhaps if you realized that the law guarantees or restricts your own personal liberty; protects or jeopardizes your health, your home, your happiness; regulates the food you eat, the clothes you wear, the books you read, the amusements you enjoy; in fact permits or prohibits your every act, you would feel a serious obligation to inquire into the nature of such authority over you. Perhaps if you knew that the booksellers of Denver reported that they had sold more books on civil government and political economy in six months after women were enfranchised in that state than in ten years before, you would be convinced that women appreciate the responsibility of voting, and prepare themselves to "administer the sacrament of citizenship" intelligently. Perhaps if you knew the overwhelming testimony from the most prominent, responsible, and respected citizens of the suffrage states agrees that woman suffrage has resulted in better candidates for office, cleaner polling places, quieter elections, and improved legislation, and that women have grown more intelligent, self-reliant, respected, and womanly under its influence, you would feel it your duty to work that such results might come to all states.[11]

Many Tennessee women have taken up Mrs. Catt's challenge. We have sent a petition to Congress along with over four hundred letters in favor of the proposed amendment.[12] Now Tennessee has the opportunity to be the concluding vote for its ratification. We invite you citizens of Nashville to join us as we reach out to the members of the Tennessee General Assembly and demand that they vote to ratify the Nineteenth Amendment. Thank you.

(The audience applauds as Kenny comes to Allen and shakes her hand. Allen returns to her seat, and Kenny comes to the podium.)

---

11. Memphis *Commercial Appeal*, October 20, 1909, quoted in Taylor, *Woman Suffrage* 30.

12. Ibid., 32.

KENNY

We have another prominent suffrage leader from Memphis today, Mrs. Lide Smith Meriwether. Mrs. Meriwether served as president of the first woman suffrage league in Tennessee, which was organized in Memphis in May 1889. Since Mrs. Meriwether is one of the chief representatives of liberal thought in Tennessee, we have asked her to share with us her reasons for favoring the enfranchisement of women. I give you Mrs. Lide Meriwether.

(While the audience applauds, Kenny returns to her seat, and Meriwether comes to the podium.)

MERIWETHER

I have often been asked why I am a suffragist, not only by men but also by women who have yet to join the movement. Perhaps, even at this late hour, there are some among you who are undecided. I will address my remarks to you.

HECKLER 1

(Remains seated but shouts)

It ain't gonna do no good.

MERIWETHER

(Ignoring him). We women demand the vote because "Being twenty-one years old, we object to being classed with minors. Born in America and loyal to [our] institutions, we protest against being made perpetual aliens. Costing the treasuries of our country nothing, we protest against acknowledging the male pauper as our political superior. Being obedient to law, we protest against the statute, which classes us with the convict and makes the pardoned criminal our political superior. Being sane, we object to being classed with lunatics. Possessing an average amount of intelligence, we protest against legal classification with the idiot. We taxpayers claim the right to representation. We married women want to own our clothes. We married breadwinners want to own our earnings. We mothers want an equal partnership in our children. We educated women want the power to offset the illiterate vote in our state."[13]

---

13. In 1895, the editor of the *Arena* magazine asked Meriwether to respond to the notion that the great majority of southern women were against the vote for women. In response, Mrs. Meriwether provided the editor with a petition naming reasons why women should want the vote, which was signed by nearly 600 women from Tennessee. Meriwether's petition appears in "Tennessee," *History of Woman Suffrage*, vol. 4, eds. Elizabeth Cady Stanton, Susan B. Anthony, Matilda Joslyn Gage, and Ida H. Harper (New York, 1881-1922) 927–928 and is quoted from Project Gutenberg EBook #29870, Chapter LXIV, 31 August 2009 <http://www.gutenberg.org/files/29870/29870-h/29870-h.htm#CHAPTER_LXIV>.

I am a proud suffragist. The yellow ribbon I wear is my suffrage badge. I wear it gladly because it stands for equal rights for women.[14] As one of the nationally recognized promoters of woman's enfranchisement, Susan B. Anthony, told us when she visited Nashville, we "cannot rest until woman's name stands for as much as a man's name, until a woman's opinion is worth as much as a man's, and that means the ballot."[15] Women must be granted the liberty to vote and to enter politics—if we choose—only then will we be true citizens of Tennessee and of the United States. Thank you.

(Members of the audience stand and applaud wildly as Kenny comes to Meriwether and shakes her hand. Meriwether returns to her seat, and Kenny comes to the podium.)

KENNY

Thank you, Mrs. Meriwether. Our next speaker is Mrs. Anne Dallas Dudley, who is one of the most influential suffragists in Tennessee. She is founder of the Nashville Suffrage

---

14. Yellow was chosen as the emblematic color for woman's suffrage movement after Kansas suffragists adopted the state symbol of the sunflower for a campaign in 1867. "Votes for Women" was printed on the silk sashes. Smithsonian National Museum of American History, 21 May 2012 <https://americanhistory.si.edu/treasures/womens-suffrage>.

15. Anthony was in Nashville in October 1897 to attend the convention of the National Council of Women of the United States. Excerpts of her speech appeared in the American [Nashville] 27 October 1897, quoted in Taylor, *Woman Suffrage Movement* 22.

League and currently serving as vice president of the National Woman Suffrage Association. Welcome, Mrs. Dudley.

(As the audience and platform speakers applaud, Dudley comes forward to the podium as Kenny goes to her seat.)

DUDLEY

Thank you, Mrs. Kenny. I am delighted to stand up for woman suffrage with you and the other platform speakers whom I admire greatly.

VERTREES

(Stands and shouts)

Ladies . . . ladies . . . before you go any further, I demand to be heard.

(Some booing from audience. Mrs. Dudley waves her hand to quieten the audience and to allow him to continue.)

I am Nashville attorney John Jacob Vertrees. I represent the men's party of the Tennessee State Association Opposed to Woman Suffrage. There are many reasons why women should not be given the vote. First of all, only those who bear arms should be allowed to vote. Secondly, as I have said in my manifesto *To the Men of Tennessee on Female Suffrage*, women are too emotional and sentimental to vote on policy matters. "A Woman's life is one of frequent and regular periods marked by mental and nervous irritability, when sometimes even her mental equilibrium is disturbed. ... [Furthermore] I do not believe that women of Tennessee want the ballot, but even if they [do] ... it is not a question of what women want, but what they ought to have, and ... it is a question for men alone to determine."[16]

(Lots of booing from the audience. Vertrees holds up his hand to quieten the audience and speaks again.)

VERTREES

Please ... please ... indulge me for one more minute. On the subject of the inappropriateness of women voting, I would like for you to hear from Miss Josephine Anderson Pearson. She is President of the Tennessee State Association Opposed to Woman Suffrage. Miss Pearson resides in Monteagle. She is visiting Nashville to lobby state legislators to vote against ratifying the Nineteenth Amendment. *(Turning to Pearson).* Miss Pearson, please tell us why you are against suffrage for women. *(He sits.)*

---

16. Quoted in Weiss 39, 40.

*(Several suffragists in audience boo her, but Pearson march-
es down front and center and speaks defiantly.)*

PEARSON

I wear this red rose to signify my opposition to woman suffrage. The anti-suffrage movement is a "Holy War, a crusade [I keep] in memory of my Mother for Southern Motherhood, through which her guiding spirit has led me all
the way!"[17] In fighting against woman suffrage, I am doing
God's will, for the Bible says that woman's place is in the
home as a loving wife and mother. *(She points to the wom-
en on stage and wags her finger at them.)* You women who
ask for the vote are ". . . modern Eve[s] [who ask] for the
forbidden fruit that may give its essence of deadly poison in
the possible disruption of home."[18] Why leave the innocent
beauty of the home to enter the deadly realm of dirty realm
of politics? As Charlotte Rowe, our beloved secretary of the
National Association Opposed to Woman Suffrage, says, ".
. . we are determined to prevent women from descending
to the political level of men, which if accomplished, will

---

17. Quoted from Elna Green, *Southern Strategies: Southern Women
and the Woman Suffrage Questions* (Chapel Hill: U North Carolina,
1997) in Pearson Papers, Tennessee Archives, 5 August 2019 <http://
www.jprof.com/2012/09/15/josephine-pearson-accomplished-and-anti-
suffrage/>.

18. Quoted in Weiss 38.

cheapen women and draw them into the mire of politics."[19] Furthermore, we believe . . . .

(Mrs. Dudley interrupts Pearson.)

DUDLEY

Madam, that is quite enough! You have had your say. Please sit down!

(Reluctantly Pearson sits, the audience applauds, and Dudley prepares to speak but is interrupted again by hecklers. The next three hecklers' speeches should be delivered in rapid succession.)

HECKLER 2

Not all women want to vote, Mrs. Dudley.

HECKLER 3

Allowing women to vote will take them away from their families. What are their children supposed to do without mothers?

---

19. Quoted in Weiss 115.

HECKLER 4

Yes, that's right. If they get to vote, women will neglect their homes.

(Audience boos the hecklers.)

DUDLEY

(Waiting for the audience to settle down, she finally speaks).

To those who believe that we should not allow women to vote because not all women want to vote, I ask, "Is that a just reason why those who need the ballot for their own protection should not have it? The ballot is not compulsory and those who wish to sit among the ashes of an old ideal while the Phoenix of the new is winging its way toward the dawn will still have the freedom of their will."[20]

To those who are against woman suffrage because it will take women "out of the home," let me first state the obvious and that is that many women work outside the home. Secondly, the assumption that "all women have comfortable, attractive homes over which they have absolute jurisdiction"

---

20. Most of Dudley's speech is excerpted from an address she gave to the Nashville Housekeeper's Club, *The Tennessean* [Nashville], 20 February 1913, quoted in Taylor, *Woman Suffrage* 41–43.

is false. Moreover, the modern woman needs the ballot to protect her home: "In days gone by she was not obligated to ask a city government to see that her water supply was pure. ... She was not obligated to ask a corrupt city council for milk inspectors in order to see that her children were not infected with typhoid or tuberculosis."

To those that say that woman will neglect her home for politics, I say, such a woman who would neglect her home for politics will probably neglect it for "bridge or something equally less vital." I predict that "the cradle will be rocked, the dishes washed, and still by feminine hands, even if women should give thirty minutes of their time a year for casting a vote."

(Applause)

HECKLER 2

(Stands)

Women don't have time to vote anyway, Mrs. Dudley.

DUDLEY

"This objection is constantly advanced by some woman who has all the time in the world to have her hair curled and her nails manicured, her gowns fitted, and [who] thinks the giving of a pink tea one of the serious things in life." Give us the opportunity to take politics seriously. Give us the vote, and we will find the time to vote.

(Much applause)

HECKLER 3

We men don't want our southern women to stain their hands with the dirty business of politics.

DUDLEY

We have heard that objection many times before from men—the southern woman is too ladylike, too delicate to venture into the filthy atmosphere of the polling place. I say give her the vote, and she will clean up the polling place! The southern woman will not "hesitate to walk up to the ballot box to vote for some measure to protect her home and children or for the protection of some little laborer or other less fortunate woman."

Just because we have men in the audience today who speak against suffrage for women, do not think we do not have male support for the woman vote. Our fathers, husbands, and brothers stand behind us, and over the years, many famous American men have stood up for us, including Thomas Paine, William Lloyd Garrison, Ralph Waldo Emerson, and Frederick Douglass.[21] Among us today are two great Tennesseans who believe in equal rights for women. I speak of Tennessee legislator from Memphis Joseph Hanover and US Congressman Thetus W. Sims. Representative Hanover says that he has always believed women should be equal to men, so he is the perfect person to serve as our suffrage floor leader in the state General Assembly when it considers ratification of the Nineteenth Amendment. We have always been able to rely on Congressman Sims to speak up for women in the US House of Representatives. Two years ago, writhing with pain from an unset broken arm and shoulder, Congressman Sims prolonged seeing a physician so that he could cast his vote for woman suffrage.[22] Representative Hanover and Congressman Sims, please stand up and be recognized.

(Hanover and Sims stand and wave to the crowd. Lots of cheering drown out the boos.)

Also, I have in my hand a letter from Memphis attorney

---

21. Brooke Kroeger, "The Little-Known Story of the Men Who Fought for Woman's Vote," *Timeline* (March 15, 2018), 22 October 2019 < https://timeline.com/the-men-who-supported-suffragettes-c8d1b921d71f>.

22. Laurine Lebrun, "7 Suffragist Men and the Importance of Allies," *Turning Point Suffragist Memorial*, 22 October 2019 < https://suffragist-memorial.org/7-suffragist-men-and-the-importance-of-allies/>.

Guston T. Fitzhugh who is not able to be with us today. You may remember that he drafted legislation in 1917 granting women the vote in Tennessee, but the bill was defeated. Mr. Fitzhugh writes, "I favor the enfranchisement of women, both by our state and nation, not only as an act of simple justice to our women but because I am firmly convinced that it will result in better laws, better officials, better government, marked improvement in social and civic conditions, and the advancement of a higher type of civilization."[23]

Yes, forward thinking men support the woman vote!

(Cheers and boos)

(Pointing to Vertrees in the audience.)

And as to Mr. Vertrees' argument against the woman vote—"because only men bear arms, only men should vote"—I say, "Yes, but women bear armies."[24]

(Laughter and applause)

In closing, please allow me to say, "I have never yet met a man or woman who denied that taxation without rep-

---

23. From the *Nashville Tennessean* 25 February 1917, quoted in Yellin and Sherman 46.

24. Ibid., 84.

resentation is tyranny. I have never yet seen one who was such a traitor to our form of government that he did not believe government rests upon the consent of the governed. This is a government of, for, and by the people, and only the law denies that women are people." Women's Votes are Women's Rights! Thank you.

(As the audience applauds, Kenny comes to Dudley. They shake hands, and Dudley returns to her seat. Kenny goes to the podium, but is interrupted by Pearson.)

PEARSON

(Stands at her seat and shouts)

You suffragists do not understand! Enfranchising women will mean the end of "the spirit of the woman of the Old South."[25] I have sent a letter to anti-suffragists in Tennessee urging them to insist that their representatives reject the Nineteenth Amendment. The Tennessee General Assembly must stand up for "State Rights, Honor, and the safety of Southern civilization."[26] Surely you must see that extending the vote to White women will give colored women the vote, too, and that will put an end to our way of life!

---

25. Quoted in Weiss 38.
26. Quoted in Weiss 130.

(Audience boos loudly and Pearson sits down.)

KENNY

(Obviously deeply disturbed by Pearson's racial prejudice, Kenny waits for Pearson to sit down before she speaks.)

As I have crossed the state in support of the vote for <u>all</u> women, I have heard the claim that we cannot enfranchise the White woman because it will enfranchise the Negro woman. I am ashamed to say that our suffrage associations have excluded colored women for fear that working with them will threaten the passage of the Nineteenth Amendment. But I am proud to report that in recent times in Nashville, White women and colored women have come together for the common good. When women were allowed to vote in last year's local elections, I conferred with colored women leaders, and with their help, we supported candidates for good government reform in Nashville.

With us today are two leaders in the Nashville Negro Community with whom I have worked for woman suffrage—Mrs. Mattie E. Coleman and Mrs. J. Frankie Pierce. Ladies, please stand.

(Coleman and Pierce stand.)

As Chairman of the Ratification Committee of the Tennessee League of Women Voters, I appointed Mrs. Coleman as State Negro Organizer and Mrs. Pierce as Secretary of Colored Suffrage Work.[27] These women are intelligent, loyal, and have a dignity that has "made new friends for their race and woman suffrage. . . . They [have] proved that they [are] trying to keep step with the march of progress and with a little patience, trust and vision, the universal tie of motherhood and sisterhood can and will overcome prejudice against them as voters."[28] Now I ask them to come forward and join us on the platform to say a few words about their work.

(As Coleman and Pierce come to the podium, platform speakers look surprised and raise their eyebrows. At the same time, White turns to Meriwether and whispers in her ear, "Did you know about this?" and Mrs. Meriwether shakes her head "no." White and Meriwether turn to Allen and whisper their disapproval. In the audience, the shocked Pearson is outraged. She mumbles under her breath, "Well, I never," looks at Vertrees, and he stands and, if possible, tosses his chair to the ground. They both storm out of the auditorium. When Coleman and Pierce arrive at the po-

---

27. Anita Shafer Goodstein, "A Rare Alliance: African American and White Women in the Tennessee Elections of 1919 and 1920," *Journal of Southern History* 64.2 (May 1998): 229.

28. Quoted in Goodstein 235-236.

*dium, they shake hands with Kenny. Kenny returns to her
seat. Standing side by side, Coleman speaks first.)*

COLEMAN

Thank you, Mrs. Kenny. My commitment to woman's suffrage is rooted in the church. As a pastor's wife, I seek a
purpose and an independent role from our husbands for
women of both Colored and Christian Methodist Episcopal Churches.[29] "Surely this is the age of women. Take the
women of the Church as a whole and they are the means
by which the Church succeeds and the gospel is promul-
gated." Outside the church, Negro women support reform
programs for all women, including pensions for mothers,
protective legislation for women and children in the labor
force, equal pay for men and women school teachers, settlement houses, <u>and</u> woman suffrage. Only in Nashville have
Tennessee colored women been invited to work with White
women on behalf of woman's enfranchisement. Working
with the Negro women's clubs in Nashville, I helped to
register us for the 1919 local election. Of the 7,500 wom-
en who registered to vote, 2,500 were Negro, and we were
22% of women voting in Nashville and Memphis. *(Look-
ing towards Kenny.)* As promised, Mrs. Kenny, we voted for
local reform candidates. All we ask in return is the White

---

29. Coleman's speech is quoted in and paraphrased from Goodstein 226-
235.

woman's support for reforms that will benefit us. We have 12,000 women organized in Tennessee who seek a vocational school for our girls. We ask that you support us, and we will support you. Thank you. *(She turns to Pierce.)* Mrs. Pierce?

(There is no applause. Coleman steps back and stands R of the podium while Pierce speaks.)

PIERCE

I am a child of slaves. My vocation is schoolteacher. My civic duty is to the advancement of colored women. I am for woman suffrage. "What will the Negro women do with the vote? We will stand by the White women. We are optimistic because we have faith in the best White women of the country, of Nashville. We are going to make you proud of us, because we are going to help [you as well as ourselves]. We are interested in the same moral uplift of the community in which we live as you are. We are asking only one thing—a square deal. . . . We want recognition in all forms of this government. We want a state vocational school for delinquent girls and a child welfare department of the state, and more room in state schools."[30] Already we see what can be

30. Quoted in Carole Stanford Bucy, "Juno Frankie Pierce," *Tennessee Encyclopedia*, 17 July 2019 <https://tennesseeencyclopedia.net/entries/juno-frankie-pierce/>.

accomplished when Negro and White women work together. I am speaking of Bethlehem House here in Nashville where educational activities for poor colored children are supported by funds from both Negro and White communities and which are administered by a board and volunteers made up of both races.

Mrs. Coleman and I, as well as our colleagues across the state, hope to join you to press for the passage of the Nineteenth Amendment in the Tennessee General Assembly. We shall not be denied the vote, for, as Negro suffragist Lottie Rollin argued in 1869 speaking to the South Carolina House of Representatives, woman's vote is a human right: "We ask. . . [for] suffrage not as favor, not as a privilege, but as a right based on the ground that we are human beings, and as such entitled to all human rights." [31] *(This quotation should be read slowly and climactically.)*

(The speakers on stage stand and burst into applause as do members of the audience. Delighted, Pierce turns to Coleman, joins arms with her, and brings her forward with her. Kenny gives the women a few seconds to take in the accolades, then motions for the speakers to join her left and right of the podium to close out the rally.)

---

31. Quoted in Terborg-Penn 45.

KENNY

Thank you, Ladies. *(She nods to speakers right and left.)* In a few days, the question of women's enfranchisement will be decided on the floor of the Tennessee General Assembly. We have conducted a poll of legislators and found that many are undecided.[32] Now is the time to act. We must let the legislators know that for the sake of our children's future, we women must have a voice in government. We must have the vote! Join our campaign today. Women's votes are <u>human</u> rights!

(Cheers from audience)

We will close out our rally by having Miss Sue White[33] lead us in a song, which is to the tune of "America." You may find the words of the song in your program.

WHITE

(White begins singing the following popular suffrage song to the tune of "America." The other speakers join in singing, as does the audience.)

---

32. Weiss 34.

33. Any one of the speakers with a good voice may lead the song.

My country 'tis of thee
To make your women free
This is our plea.
High have our hopes been raised
In these enlightened days
That for her justice praised
Our land might be.
My native country thee
Grant us equality!
Then shall we see
In this fair land of light
Justice and truth and right
Ruling instead of might
Trust liberty.[34]

At the close of the song, the platform speakers pick up their signs and begin chanting, "Votes for Women, Votes for Women." They encourage the audience to join in.

Pierce, Allen, and Meriwether march off the stage down the left auditorium aisle, shaking hands as they go with members of the audience wearing yellow roses. Dudley, Kenny, and Coleman march off the stage down the right auditorium aisle, shaking hands as they go with members of the

---

34. *News Scimitar* [Memphis], 4 May 1914, quoted in Taylor, *Woman Suffrage* 132.

audience wearing yellow roses.

Everyone continues to chant "Votes for Women" as the speakers march out the auditorium doors. Meanwhile, several members of the audience throw off their red roses!

THE END

Property List

Five straight back chairs

Old-fashion speakers' podium

Two stage banners (white, purple, and gold) that read "VOTES FOR WOMEN!"

Seven or more yellow suffrage sashes that read "VOTES FOR WOMEN"

Five suffrage costumes for Kenny, Dudley, White, Allen, and Meriwether: hats and white dresses authentic to 1920 draped with suffrage sashes

1920 period costumes for Coleman, Pierce, Suffrage Leader, Vertrees, Pearson, and Hecklers (attendees may be encouraged to dress in historical costumes)

Letter from Guston T. Fitzhugh for Dudley

Seven or more suffrage signs:
"Colored Women for the Vote"
"Negro Women are Suffragists, Too"
"Women's votes are women's rights!"
"No more tyranny!"
"We demand the vote!"
"Women are men's equal!"
"Give us the vote!"

Six or more anti-suffrage signs
"Women's vote will feminize men!"
"Women's votes will masculinize women!"
"Women belong in the home, not in the ballot box!"
"No votes for Women!"
"Down with the 19th Amendment!"
"No Votes for Negro Women!"

Seven or more suffrage fans. See example at
https://americanhistory.si.edu/collections/search/
object/nmah_516788

Suffrage and anti-suffrage literature handouts. For cartoons and broadsides, see examples at https://sharetngov.tnsosfiles.com/tsla/exhibits/suffrage/struggle.htm

Lyrics of the suffrage song should be printed in the program for the audience. To hear the song sung, see https://networks.h-net.org/node/2289/links/174999/suffrage-song-sung-tune-america.

SUFFRAGISTS FEATURED IN *TENNESSEE WOMEN FOR THE VOTE*

Martha Elizabeth Moore Allen (1851-1936)

Martha Elizabeth Moore Allen was born on November 16, 1851, in Plymouth, Indiana, where she later attended girls' schools and married Jacob Davis Allen.[35] Allen came to believe in women's enfranchisement when she heard Susan B. Anthony speak at a rally in the 1870s; however, she did not act on her conviction until she was able to get away

35. Allen's biography is compiled from "Martha E. Allen," *The J.B. Mann Suffrage Collection,* The Digital Archive of Memphis Public Libraries, 10 October 2019 <https://cdm16108.contentdm.oclc.org/digital/collection/p13039coll1/id/191> and Yellin and Sherman, *The Perfect 36.*

from her anti-feminist father-in-law when she and her husband moved from Indiana to Tennessee in 1889. Once in Tennessee, she became a leader in the suffrage movement both in Memphis and across the state.

In 1906, Allen founded the Equal Suffrage League and served as its president until 1912. She was also a member of the Memphis League of Women Voters, which was an offshoot of the woman suffrage movement. Allen was known for her organizational skills and her speaking and writing abilities. She was often called on to organize suffrage events, speak at parades and rallies, and write newspaper pieces.

Like many conservative suffragists, Allen (a Christian Scientist) endorsed prohibition and worked for the ratification of the Eighteenth Amendment of the US Constitution, which banned the sale and drinking of alcohol in the United States. By the time she settled in Memphis in 1898, a chapter of the Women's Christian Temperance Union (WCTU) had already been active in the city for nearly twenty-five years. She became prominent in the chapter, representing Memphis at several national meetings of the organization.[36]

---

36. The Eighteenth Amendment was ratified and took effect in 1919, but was repealed in 1933, the only amendment ever to be overturned.

After a long career as a political activist, Allen died at age eighty-seven.

⌣⟶

Mattie E. Coleman
(1870-1942)

Dr. Mattie Elizabeth Coleman was born July 3, 1870, in Sumner County, Tennessee.[37] She was a woman of many "firsts." In 1906, she graduated from Meharry Medical College (Nashville, Tennessee) and became one of the first African American women to practice medicine; in 1909 she was named the first dean of women at Lane College (Jackson, Tennessee); and in 1932 she was the first graduate to earn a degree in dentistry at Meharry. In addition, Coleman was the first Black woman to serve as state tuberculosis advisor.

---

37. Coleman's biography is compiled from Terriana Jones, Kalie Rials, Kobe Walker, and Maria Kanu, "Biography of Mattie E. Coleman," *Biographical Database of Black Women Suffragists*, 12 October 2019 <https://search.alexanderstreet.com/advanced-search>; and Jessie Carney Smith and Shirelle Phelps, "Mattie E. Coleman," *Notable American Black Women, Book II* (Detroit: Gale Research Inc., 1992): 125-28, Google Books 12 October 2019 <https://books.google.com/advanced_book_search?q>.

The daughter of a Christian minister, Coleman's religious convictions were formed at an early age. When she married Reverend P. J. Coleman in 1902 and joined the Colored Methodist Episcopal Church (CME), Coleman was not content to be a passive pastor's wife. She demanded a leadership role separate from her husband and, in so doing, promoted woman's independent and important role in the church. In 1918, she helped found the CME Woman's Connectional Council, which raised funds for Home missions. Coleman served twenty years as the council's first president.

Coleman's contributions to the Black community went beyond the church. She provided medical services to the needy and educational opportunities for poor children through her sponsorship of the Bethlehem House settlement in Nashville. In 1939, she became superintendent of the Tennessee Vocational School for Girls in Nashville, a position she held until her death.

A feminist, Coleman supported the Nineteenth Amendment to the US Constitution and knew that she could be an asset in the woman vote campaign. Having contacts in the Nashville White community, Coleman "may have initiated the biracial alliance" with suffragist Catherine Talty Kenny.[38] Certainly, she served the alliance efforts well by registering

38. Goodstein, "A Rare Alliance" 225.

over 2,500 Black women to vote in the 1919 municipal election.

Coleman died at the age of seventy-three on August 12, 1942, and is buried in Nashville.

⟨‿⟩

Anne Dallas Dudley
(1876-1955)

Anne Dallas Dudley was born into a prominent Nashvillian family on November 13, 1876.[39] She attended Ward Seminary High School and Price's College for Young Ladies (both in Nashville). In 1902, she married banker Guilford Dudley. The couple had two children.

Dudley went against upper-class society when she joined campaigns for the woman vote. In 1911, she helped form the Nashville Equal Suffrage League and served as its first

---

39. Dudley's biography is compiled from "Anne Dallas Dudley," *Turning Point: Suffragist Memorial,* 13 October 2019 <https://suffragistmemorial.org/why-the-suffragist-memorial/>; "Anne Dallas Dudley," *National Women's Hall of Fame,* 13 October 2019 <https://www.womenofthehall.org/inductee/anne-dallas-dudley/>; and Yellin and Sherman, *The Perfect 36.*

president. She was elected president of the Tennessee Equal Suffrage Association in 1915. Her leadership was instrumental in getting a bill approved by the Tennessee General Assembly to allow women to vote in presidential and municipal elections. In 1917, she was elected third vice-president of the National American Woman Suffrage Association (NAWSA), which called on her to speak on the behalf of the woman vote throughout the United States. At home in Tennessee, Dudley, along with Catherine Talty Kenny and Abby Crawford, led the campaign to ratify the Nineteenth Amendment to the US Constitution.

After the amendment was ratified and the vote for women was won, Dudley stayed active in politics. In 1920, she made a seconding speech at the Democratic National Convention in San Francisco as the first woman delegate-at-large. She helped organize the Woman's Civic League of Nashville and was president of the Maternal Welfare Organization of Tennessee.

Dudley is the most honored of Tennessee suffragists. She is one of three women featured in the Tennessee Woman Suffrage Memorial in Knoxville.[40] Her portrait hangs with

---

40. The other suffragists honored with the Knoxville memorial are Lizzie Crozier French of Knoxville and Elizabeth Avery Meriwether of Memphis.

other prominent Tennesseans in the state capitol.[41] She was inducted in the National Women's Hall of Fame in 1955. More recently, she is depicted as one of five suffragists in Alan LeQuire's monument that stands in Centennial Park in Nashville.[42] A boulevard in Nashville is named after her and a proposed park in Nashville is to be named in her honor.

Dudley died unexpectedly in 1955 and is buried in her beloved Nashville.

⌣⟶

Catherine Talty Kenny
(1874-1950)

Catherine Talty Kenny was born in 1874 in a section of Chattanooga known as Irish Hill, a poor Catholic neigh-

---

41. The portrait is entitled "The Pride of Tennessee," a 6x8 foot oil painting displayed on the first floor of the Tennessee State Capitol in the Old Supreme Court Room. The painting was proclaimed the state's official bicentennial portrait by Gov. Ned McWherter in 1990.

42. LeQuire's monument was unveiled on August 26, 2016, in celebration of Women's Equality Day. Dudley shares the spotlight with Carrie Chapman Catt, Abby Crawford Milton, Juno Frankie Pierce, and Sue Shelton White.

borhood.[43] Her father died when Kenny was four years old, leaving her mother with six children to rear alone. Kenny finished one year of high school, but dropped out to help her family. For the next ten years, she worked menial jobs before marrying John M. Kenny. The couple moved from Chattanooga when her husband started the Coca Cola bottling company in Nashville.

As the couple's financial standing improved, so did their social status and Kenny's desire to promote women's rights. By 1913, Kenny was a member of the Nashville Suffrage League and quickly became a leader in the suffrage movement around the state, joining Chattanooga's Abby Crawford Milton in organizing suffrage clubs in rural areas. In 1914, she organized a suffrage parade in Nashville, the first of its kind in the South, and in 1919 she successfully lobbied state legislators to pass a bill allowing women to vote in municipal elections.

A mother of four, Kenny often said her interest in politics stemmed from being a mother, a role she had in common with African American women with whom she collaborated. The "deal" she struck with J. Frankie Pierce and Mattie

43. Kenny's biography is compiled from Carole Stanford Bucy, "Biographical Sketch of Catherine Talty Kenny," *Biographical Database of NAWSA Suffragists, 1890-1920*, 21 October 2019 <https://documents. alexanderstreet.com/d/1009932459> and Goodstein, "A Rare Alliance" 224-225.

Coleman (she promised to support a vocational school for Black girls if they promised to vote for her progressive candidates in the 1919 election) was remarkable for its time.

Perhaps, Kenny's greatest contribution to the campaign for the woman vote was her persuading Governor Roberts to call a special session of the Tennessee General Assembly in August 1920 to consider ratifying the Nineteenth Amendment to the US Constitution, the consequence of which was winning the vote for women. After her husband's death in 1927, Kenny moved from Tennessee and lived her final years in Brooklyn, New York.

Kenny died in 1950 and is buried in the Catholic Cemetery in Brooklyn.

Lide Smith Meriwether
(1829-1913)

Lide Smith Meriwether was born in Columbus, Ohio, on October 16, 1829, and died at the age of eighty-three in

Haverstraw, New York, on September 28, 1913.[44] She graduated from the Emma Willard Seminary in Pennsylvania and
taught school in Memphis before she married Niles Meriwether in 1856. The couple had three daughters.

Meriwether was a first-generation feminist and political
activist. Her first campaign on behalf of women was waged
for prostitutes with her publication of *Soundings* (1872), a
periodical that portrayed prostitutes as victims and recognized the double standard for these "fallen women" and
the men who visited them. Acknowledging that temperance
was in part a woman's issue because drunkenness destroyed
the family, in the 1880s Meriwether traveled the state organizing chapters of the Women's Christian Temperance Union (WCTU). Besides lobbying for prohibition, Meriwether
campaigned for raising the legal age of consent, insisted
that the Memphis Police Department hire a police matron,
and demanded suffrage for women.

Meriwether was a pioneer in the woman suffrage move-

---

44. Meriwether's biography is compiled from Anita S. Goodstein, "Lide
Smith Meriwether," *Tennessee Encyclopedia*, 18 October 2019 <https://
tennesseeencyclopedia.net/entries/lide-smith-meriwether>; "Elizabeth
Avery Meriwether and Lide Smith Meriwether," *Women of Achievement*,
19 October 2019 <http://www.womenofachievement.org/heritage/
elizabeth-avery-meriwether-and-lide-smith-meriwether/>; and Yellin and
Sherman, *The Perfect 36.*

ment.[45] Early on, she organized a Woman Suffrage League in Memphis (1889) and then traveled the state organizing Equal Rights Clubs in Nashville, Knoxville, Jackson, Greenville, and Murfreesboro. Members of the Tennessee Equal Suffrage Association recognized Meriwether for her devotion to the cause in 1990 when, after serving several terms as its president, she was named their "Honorary President for Life." However, Meriwether's influence in the movement went beyond the boundaries of Tennessee. In 1892 she and women from twenty-seven states testified on behalf of woman suffrage before a committee of the US House of Representatives in Washington, DC.

Meriwether's argument for the woman vote was the foundation of the suffrage movement. As non-voters, women were classified with minors, aliens, paupers, criminals, and idiots. Not allowing women to vote perpetuated other discriminations against them, such as preventing them from owning property and having custody of their children.

Unfortunately, Meriwether died in 1913, seven years before the fruition of her fight for the woman vote was won in 1920.

---

45. Lide Smith Meriwether is often confused with her sister-in-law Elizabeth Avery Meriwether, who was also an early suffragist.

J. Frankie Pierce

(c.1864-1954)

Juno Frankie Pierce was born in Nashville in 1863 (or 1864) to an African American mother who was a house slave to Colonel Robert Allen, a member of the US House of Representatives.[46] Pierce's father was freedman Frank Seay. After attending the Roger Williams University in Nashville, she taught at Belview School, a public school for Black children. She married Clement J. Pierce and moved with him to Texas but returned to Nashville after his death.

Back in Nashville, Pierce soon became a leader in efforts to improve the welfare of Black citizens. She founded the Negro Women's Reconstruction League (for which she served as president) and the Nashville Federation of Colored Women's Clubs. An example of Pierce's activism

---

46. Pierce's biography compiled from Carol Stanford Bucy, "Juno Frankie Pierce" *Tennessee Encyclopedia*, 19 October 2019 <https://tennesseeencyclopedia.net/entries/juno-frankie-pierce/>; Rebecca Price, "Song of the Suffrage Siren: The Tennessee Women Who Bribed, Backstabbed, and Battled for the Ratification of the 19th Amendment," *Nashville Lifestyles Magazine* (Historical Issue, 2015), 05 August 2019 <https://chickhistory.org/2016/01/25/song-of-the-suffrage-siren/>; and Yellin and Sherman, *The Perfect 36*.

is a march she led to demand public restrooms in downtown Nashville for Black women.[47] She also successfully lobbied for a state-supported vocational school for delinquent Black girls who otherwise were being jailed. When the state established the Tennessee Vocational School for Colored Girls in 1921, Pierce became its first superintendent.

Pierce was committed to the woman suffrage movement because she believed the ballot would advance African American women. She and Mattie E. Coleman gladly joined forces with White suffragist Catherine Talty Kenny in support of progressive candidates in the 1919 Nashville local elections; she and Coleman registered Black women voters in turn for Kenny's promise to support a vocational school for African American girls. Their collaboration was such a success that Kenny invited Pierce to speak at the May 1920 state suffrage convention held at the Tennessee State Capitol building. On the subject of what Black women would do with the vote, Pierce pledged to stand with White women and said that Black women wanted to be recognized in all forms of government.

Pierce retired as superintendent of the Tennessee Vocational School in 1939. In 1952, she chaired the Black community's building fund for a branch of the YMCA. Pierce

---

47. As a result of the march, Montgomery Ward installed restrooms for its Black female customers.

died in Nashville in 1954. She is immortalized as one of five suffragists in Alan LeQuire's tribute monument that stands in Centennial Park in Nashville. Soon a greenspace in Nashville will be named Pierce Park in her honor.

Sue Shelton White
(1887-1943)

Sue Shelton White (also known as "Miss Sue") was born on May 25, 1887, in Henderson, Tennessee.[48] She was the sixth of seven children born to James Shelton White and Mary Callista (Swain) White. White's father died when she was nine; her mother when she was fourteen. With the help of her guardian aunt, White continued her education, earning degrees from Henderson's Georgie Robertson Christian College in 1904 and West Tennessee Business College in 1905. She served as the court reporter for the Tennessee Supreme Court in Jackson, 1907 to 1918.

---

48. White's biography is compiled from Betty Sparks Huehls, "Sue Shelton Sparks," *Tennessee Encyclopedia*, 19 October 2019 <https://tennesseeencyclopedia.net/entries/sue-shelton-white/>; "Sue Shelton White," *Turning Point Suffragist Memorial*, 20 October 2019 <https://suffragist-memorial.org/sue-shelton-white-1887-1943/>; and Yellin and Sherman, *The Perfect 36.*

White joined the Tennessee Equal Suffrage Association in 1912, and almost immediately began serving as its recording secretary. By 1918, White was dissatisfied with the passive approach of Tennessee suffragists. She moved to Washington, DC, and joined the National Woman's Party (NWP) known for its more radical practices. There she edited the organization's newspaper, the *Suffragist*. Soon she took on more controversial activities. She was arrested after burning President Woodrow Wilson in effigy and jailed for five days in the dilapidated Old Work House. After being released, she traveled around the country via railroad car (the "Prison Special") lobbying for woman suffrage.

Nineteen twenty found White in Nashville where she was instrumental in organizing suffragists to push the Tennessee General Assembly to ratify the Nineteenth Amendment of the US Constitution. Her efforts were successful. The legislators ratified the amendment by one vote, making Tennessee the last state needed to ratify the amendment and give women the vote.

After the suffrage campaign, White earned a law degree from Washington College of Law in Washington, DC, in 1923. That same year she helped to write the Equal Rights Amendment (ERA) to the US Constitution sponsored by the NWP.[49] White returned to Jackson where she practiced law from 1926 to 1930 and continued to be active in the Democratic Party. Under Franklin D. Roosevelt's administration, White was appointed to positions in the Consumers Division of the National Recovery Administration (NRA) and the Social Security Administration.

White died on May 6, 1943, after a long battle with cancer. She is one of the five suffragists depicted in Alan Le-Quire's tribute monument that stands in Centennial Park in Nashville.

---

49. The ERA proposed to guarantee equal rights for all American citizens regardless of sex. The amendment has never been adopted despite many efforts over the years. In 1972, Tennessee voted to ratify the amendment but rescinded that action in 1974. Twenty-five states (Tennessee is not among them) have approved changes to their state constitutions that say their citizens cannot be denied equal rights because of sex.

SELECTED BIBLIOGRAPHY

Casey, Paula F. "Four Prominent Tennessee Suffragists." *Tennessee Women of Vision and Courage.* Eds. Charlotte Crawford and Ruth Johnson Smiley. North Charleston: CreateSpace, 2013. 47-57.

Goodstein, Anita Shafer. "A Rare Alliance: African American and White Women in the Tennessee Elections of 1919 and 1920." *Journal of Southern History* 64.2 (May 1998): 219-246.

Green, Elna Green. *Southern Strategies: Southern Women and the Woman Suffrage Questions.* Chapel Hill: U North Carolina, 1997.

Kroeger, Brooks. "The Little-Known Story of the Men Who Fought for Woman's Vote." *Timeline* (March 15, 2018), 22 October 2019 < https://timeline.com/the-men-who-supported-suffragettes-c8d1b921d71f>.

Sawyer, Susan. *More than Petticoats: Remarkable Tennessee Women.* Helena, Montana: Falcon, 2000.

Taylor, A. Elizabeth. *The Woman Suffrage Movement in Tennessee.* New York: Bookman, 1957.

Terborg-Penn, Rosalyn. *African American Women in the Struggle for the Vote, 1850-1920.* Bloomington: U of Indiana P, 1998.

Weiss, Elaine. *The Woman's Hour: The Great Fight to Win the Vote.* New York: Penguin, 2019.

Wheeler, Marjorie Spruill, ed. *Votes for Women! The Woman Suffrage Movement in Tennessee, the South, and the Nation.* Knoxville: U of Tennessee, 1955.

Yellin, Carol Lynn, and Janann Sherman. *The Perfect 36: Tennessee Delivers Woman Suffrage.* Oak Ridge: Iris, 1998.

ACKNOWLEDGEMENTS

The first version of *Tennessee Women for the Vote* was written and performed for the celebration of National Women's History Month at Middle Tennessee State University in the late 1980s. Subsequent performances were staged for meetings of AAUW Murfreesboro Branch and AAUW of Tennessee. Many thanks to my friends and colleagues who took roles in these early productions.

I am grateful to Charlotte Crawford and Ruth Johnson Smiley for giving me an opportunity to revise the play for inclusion in their *Tennessee Women of Vision and Courage* and for their steadfast encouragement along the journey to its publication in 2013.

I am now indebted to Charlotte and Ruth once again for this publication of the third version of the play for which I have done extensive revision just in time for the centennial celebration of the passage of the Nineteenth Amendment of the US Constitution in 2020.

A primary difference between the third version of *Tennessee Women for the Vote* and earlier versions is the inclusion of African American women. Too often in our admiration of suffragist women, we have overlooked the stories of Black women and their contributions to the suffrage movement. My play includes two of those stories.

For motivating my desire to explore Black women in the suffrage movement, I am thankful to Rebecca Price and Chick History, Inc., a nonprofit organization dedicated to rebuilding history to include women "one story at a time" <https://chickhistory.org/>. Thanks, Rebecca!

ABOUT LICENSING

PLEASE NOTE: ***Tennessee Women for the Vote: A Suffrage Play, 1920,*** like all plays, is subject to a licensing fee—regardless of the size of the audience or whether or not an admission fee is charged.

No part of this book may be reproduced, stored in a retrieval system, or transmitted in any form, by any means including mechanical, electronic, photocopying, recording, videotaping, or otherwise, without the prior written permission of the Tennessee Women Project. (Yes, photocopying a script is illegal.)

ABOUT THE AUTHOR

B. Ayne Cantrell, DA, (Professor Emerita, Middle Tennessee State University) retired from MTSU in 2005 where she taught Shakespeare's tragedies and women's drama for over thirty years. At MTSU Ayne was recognized for her contributions to the advancement of women at the university with the King-Hampton Award (1991) and the Women's Studies Ayne Cantrell Award (1992). For a number of years, she served as president, director, and actor for the Murfreesboro Ensemble Theatre. *Tennessee Women for the Vote* is Ayne's first published play. Its subject—an imagined rally for woman suffrage based on historical fact—is a natural offshoot of her work in community and academic theatre, study of women's history and literature, and her lifelong devotion to pursuing women's rights.

Made in the USA
Monee, IL
19 March 2020